Also by Rachael Reed

Sis
Sis 2 Blood on the Streets

Standalone
Codefendant
Codefendant
Once a Cheater
Once a Cheater
Passport Bro
What Happens in Prison
Preference
Sprinkle Sprinkle
Championship Bad
Street Exodus
Street Exodus
Street Royalty
Pawns of Power
SIS
Cartel Bloodline
Get Money Girls
Skip the Games
Til Death Do Us Part

Backpage Hustle
Link in Bio
The Virgin and The Kingpin
A Gangsta's Heart
Boosters
Can't Turn a Hoe Into a Housewife
Better you Than Me
Wig Dealer: How to Start Your wig Business

Wig Dealer
How to Start Your Wig Business

Rachael Reed
©2024

Chapter 1 Getting Started How to Start Your Hair Business

Getting Started

Hi, welcome to your new journey! This guide will help you start your hair business with little to no resources. Your journey to financial independence and entrepreneurial success begins now. In this book, you will find everything you need to launch your own online hair store, including a comprehensive vendor list. You can check out the vendor list after setting up your website, but for now, let's get started on the essentials.

Step 1: Sign Up for Shopify First, you'll need to sign up for Shopify. Click the link

Make sure to choose the 'Shopify' plan to access all the necessary features for your store: https://www.shopify.com/free-trial

Step 2: Upload our Shopify website template and start designing your website. It's easy and all the instructions are included. All you need is Canva. There are several FREE Shopify store templates included along with a Shopify Theme Guide that will help you in this book. See Chapter 7.

Step 3: Contact Vendors After your store setup is underway, make initial contact with the vendors listed Chapter 6. Let them know about your intentions to start drop shipping or selling online and arrange the purchase of samples if necessary. This step is crucial to ensure the quality of your products.

Step 4: Marketing and Order Fulfillment Once your store is built, refer to the marketing instructions included in this book in Chapter 2. This chapter will help you attract and retain customers. Finally, follow the step-by-step guide on how to fulfill orders to ensure a smooth operation.

Adding Products

Welcome to the next step in launching your hair store! Follow this step-by-step to add your chosen hair products to your Shopify store, set prices, manage stock, and optimize your listings to attract customers.

Step 1: Log In to Your Shopify Admin 1. Go to your Shopify admin page. 2. Log in with your credentials.

Step 2: Add a New Product 1. In the left-hand menu, click on Products. 2. Click on

Add product in the top right corner.

Step 3: Enter Product Details

1. Title: Enter a descriptive and catchy name for your product (e.g., "Brazilian Body

Wave Bundle").

2. Description: Write a detailed product description. Include important information

such as the type of hair, length, weight, color, and any other unique selling points.

Make it engaging and informative. You can use ChatGPT to help craft compelling

product descriptions that are optimized for SEO.

Step 3: Enter Product Details use ChatGPT to help craft compelling product descriptions that are optimized for SEO.

Step 4: Add High-Quality Images

1. Images: Click on Add image to upload high-quality images of the hair bundles. Use photos you have or find high-quality images online that closely match your products.

2. Ensure the images are clear, well-lit, and show different angles of the hair.

Step 5: Set Prices and Manage Stock

1. Pricing: Price: Set your initial price with about a 10% profit margin to attract

customers. For example, if your cost is $50, set the price around $55. Compare price: Optionally, set a higher price to show that your product is on sale.

2. Inventory: SKU: Enter a unique stock- keeping unit (SKU) for tracking. (You can

just write 100)

Step 6: Manage Shipping Choose how long it will take to ship your product within a reasonable timeframe.

Step 7: Optimize for SEO 1. Search engine listing preview: Page title: Use a keyword-rich title. You can use ChatGPT to generate effective SEO tags and keywords. Meta description: Write a brief, engaging summary of the product.

Step 8: Save Your Product

Click on Save to add the product to your store.

Step 9: Repeat for Additional

Products Repeat steps 2-8 for each hair product you want to add to your store.

· · · ·

TIPS FOR SUCCESS

● High-Quality Images: Always use the best quality images you can find. If possible, take your own photos once you receive samples.

● Detailed Descriptions: The more information you provide, the more

confident customers will feel about their purchase. Include texture, length, color,

and care instructions.

● Attractive Pricing: Start with competitive pricing to build a customer base. Once you have repeat customers and positive reviews, gradually increase your prices.

enhance your store's visibility online.

FULFILLING ORDERS

Step 1: Receive the Order Notification

1. When a customer places an order, you'll receive a notification from Shopify.

2. Go to your Shopify admin and click on Orders to see the new order details.

Step 2: Contact Your Vendor

Notify the Vendor: Contact your vendor with the order details. Make sure they have all the necessary information, including the product type, quantity, and customer's shipping address.

Payment: Complete the payment to your vendor for the order.

Step 3: Vendor Ships the Product

1. Direct Shipping: Your vendor will ship the product directly to your customer. Ensure the vendor knows to send you the tracking number once the product is shipped.

2. Receive Tracking Number: Once the vendor ships the order, they will provide you with a tracking number.

Step 4: Update Tracking Information in Shopify

1. In your Shopify admin, go to Orders.

2. Click on the specific order you need to update.

3. In the order details page, click Add tracking.

4. Enter the tracking number provided by your vendor.

5. Select the shipping carrier from the drop- down menu.

6. Click Save.

WIG DEALER: HOW TO START YOUR WIG BUSINESS

Receiving Products for Content Creation

Sometimes, it's beneficial to receive the products yourself before shipping them to

your customers. This allows you to create content for your social media channels,

showcasing the products in use.

1. Notify the Vendor: Let the vendor know to ship the products to you first.

2. Create Content: Once you receive the products, create engaging content for

Instagram, TikTok, and other platforms. Show off the product's quality, how to use it, and styling tips.

3.Repackage and Ship: After creating content, repackage the product and ship it to your customer. Ensure you provide the customer with the new tracking number.

Step 5: Communicate with Your Customer

1.Order Confirmation: Send an email to your customer confirming their order and letting them know it's being processed.

2. Shipping Confirmation: Once you have the tracking number, send another email to the customer with the tracking information. This keeps them informed and reassures them that their order is on its way.

Step 6: Brand Your Products (Optional) Some vendors offer branding services. This means they can add your logo and packaging to the products

before shipping them to your customers.

1. Discuss Branding Options: Talk to your vendor about available branding options.

2. Provide Branding Materials: If required, provide your vendor with your logo and any other branding materials.

3. Confirm Branding Details: Make sure to confirm all branding details before placing the order to ensure consistency.

Tips for Success

● Timely Communication: Always keep your customer updated about their order status.

Timely communication builds trust and enhances the customer experience.

● High-Quality Content: When creating content, use high-quality images and videos to showcase your products effectively.

● Customer Service: Be responsive to any customer inquiries or concerns. Excellent

customer service can turn a one-time buyer into a repeat customer. By following these steps, you'll ensure a smooth order fulfillment process, keeping your customers happy and coming back.

. . . .

CUSTOMER SERVICE

Customer service is the backbone of any successful business, especially when running an online store. Here's how you can provide exceptional customer service and set up a dedicated email address for your store.

Setting Up a Dedicated Email Address

1. Choose an Email Provider: Select an email provider that suits your needs. Popular options include Gmail, Outlook, or consider using a custom domain email for a professional touch.

2. Create Your Email Address: Set up your email address specifically for your store. For example, abchair@example.com or mary@abchair.com

3. Linking Your Email on Shopify:

Step 1: Log in to your Shopify admin panel.

Step 2: Go to Settings > General.

Step 3: Scroll down to the Store details section.

Step 4: In the Store contact email field, enter your newly created email address.

Step 5: Click Save to update the changes.

Now, your customers can reach out to you directly via this email address for any inquiries, concerns, or feedback related to their orders or products. Providing Good Customer Service

1. Timely Responses: Aim to respond to customer inquiries as quickly as possible, ideally within 24 hours. Prompt responses show customers that you value their time and concerns.

2. Personalization: Address customers by their names and personalize your responses whenever feasible. This creates a more engaging and pleasant customer experience.

3. Clear Communication: Ensure all communication is clear and concise. Provide

detailed information about products, shipping times, and any other relevant details.

4. Problem Resolution: If a customer has an issue, handle it promptly and professionally. Offer solutions or alternatives to resolve the problem

satisfactorily.

5. Follow-Up: Follow up with customers after their purchase to ensure they are satisfied with their products. This gesture demonstrates your

commitment to their satisfaction.

6. Feedback Collection: Encourage customers to leave reviews and feedback. Use this information to improve your products and services continually.

Conclusion By setting up a dedicated email address and providing excellent customer service, you're laying the foundation for a positive and trustworthy relationship with your customers. Happy customers are more likely to return and recommend your products to others, contributing to the growth and success of your

company. Remember, each interaction is an opportunity to build loyalty and strengthen your brand reputation. Invest time and effort in delivering exceptional customer service—it's a worthwhile investment in the long-term success of your business.

WIG DEALER: HOW TO START YOUR WIG BUSINESS

Essentials

Now that you've signed up for Shopify and chosen your plan, let's move on to setting up your store. This part will guide you through buying a domain, using Shopify templates for policies, setting up Shopify Payments, and connecting your bank account using Plaid.

Step 1: Buy a Domain on Shopify: Definition of a Domain A domain is your website's unique address on the internet. It's what people type into their web browsers to find your online store, like "abchair.com".

1. Log in to your Shopify admin.

2. Go to Settings > Domains.

3. Click Buy new domain.

4. Enter the domain name you want and check its availability.

5. If the domain is available, follow the prompts to purchase it.

6. Shopify will automatically configure your new domain to work with your store

Step 3: Set Up Your Store Policies

1. In your Shopify admin, go to Settings > Policies.

2. Use Shopify's template options for:

○ Refund policy

○ Privacy policy

○ Terms of service

Review the templates and customize them as needed to suit your business.

4. Click Save to apply the policies to your store.

Step 4: Set Up Shopify Payments

1. In your Shopify admin, go to Settings > Payments.

2. In the Shopify Payments section, click Complete account setup.

3. Enter the required business information, including your business type and tax details.

4. Click Save.

Step 5: Connect Your Bank Account Using Plaid

1. During the Shopify Payments setup, you will be prompted to link your bank account.

2. Select Use Plaid to connect your bank account securely.

3. Choose your bank from the list or use the search function to find it.

4. Enter your online banking credentials to connect your account via Plaid.

5. Verify your bank account details and complete the connection process.

Chapter 2 Marketing and Branding Your Hair and Wig Business

Here's how you can use these platforms to showcase your bundles, wigs, and lashes, and get those sales rolling in.

Step 1: Understand Your Audience First things first, know who you're talking to. Your audience loves hair that looks good and feels good, and they're scrolling through their feeds for inspo, trends, and tips. Your job? Catch their eye and make them stop scrolling.

Step 2: Create Engaging Content Here's how you do it:

1. Play with Trends: Keep an eye on what's trending. Whether it's a dance challenge, a catchy song, or a new filter, hop on the trend and put

your spin on it with your hair products. Show off those luscious locks in creative ways.

2. Show Off Your Hair: Create videos where you play with the hair. Run your fingers through it, show how it moves, and flaunt those sleek finishes. Give your audience a close-up of the texture and shine.

3. Transformation Videos: People love seeing before-and-after transformations. Start with your natural hair and then switch to your bundles or wigs. Show how easy it is to change your look and slay the day.

4. Tutorials and Tips: Share styling tips, how to install the wigs, or the best way to care for the bundles. Position yourself as the go-to expert for all things hair.

Step 3: Use Hashtags and Captions

1.Hashtags: Use popular and relevant hashtags

like #HairGoals, #BundleDeals, #WigLife, #HairTransformation, and #ABCBeauty.

2. Captions: Keep your captions engaging and ask questions to boost interaction. For example, "Which look do you love more? ◈ Let me know!" or "Ever wondered how to get that flawless wave? Watch this!"

Step 4: Collaborate with Influencers

Find Influencers: Use platforms like BeautyClout to find influencers who can help promote your products. Look for those who align with your brand and have a strong following.

2. Send Samples: Sometimes it's worth sending your products to influencers. Let

them experience your hair bundles, wigs, and lashes firsthand.

3. Collaborate on Content: Work with influencers to create content that feels authentic and reaches a wider audience.

Step 5: Post Consistently

1. Schedule Posts: Consistency is key. Schedule your posts to keep your audience

engaged.

2. Mix It Up: Keep your content diverse. Post a mix of product showcases, tutorials, user-generated content, and trend-based videos.

Step 6: Monitor and Adjust

Analytics: Use the analytics tools on TikTok and Instagram to see what's working and what's not. Look at the views, likes, comments, and shares.

Adjust Your Strategy: If a particular type of content is performing well, create more of it. Don't be afraid to tweak your strategy based on the feedback you're getting. Examples to Get You Started.

5 Steps to Market & Sell Your Wigs

1. Build Trust

You want your customer to trust you first! In order to build trust with your audience /customer you must give to them first. Give them knowledge about wigs /products, Give them behind the scene footage and give them ALL OF THAT content IN A WAY THAT THEY will love! If you have a dope personality and love to engage, give them you!

1. Use Pain Points

WIG DEALER: HOW TO START YOUR WIG BUSINESS

Have you ever heard of pain points? Pain points are your customers problems. What problem are they trying to fix when purchasing your wigs?

If you take a look at the type of customers we named on the previous page,

you should be able to identify their pain points.

1. Address Their Fears

No one wants to get scammed online. Its one of the reasons alot of women
are hesitant when purchasing wigs. when a cutomer sends an email or dm to
you, answer their questions and be as truthful as possible. your website
will also address these fears in the policy section. you can also address
these fears by posting customer comments and reviews on your social
media pages.

1. Put the People Before Profits

Your profits come after you genuinely help people. your potential
customer knows you're the expert so they will ask you questions about the
type of wig they should purchase based on their situation. dont attempt to
sell them one of your higher priced wigs to fatten your pockets. sell them

the wig that really addresses their problem. This builds trust and attracts

repeat buyers.

1. Assume the Sale

most of your customers will go straight to your website to purchase

without contacting you but if they do reach out to you, answer their

questions and say "Thanks for doing business with me" once they tell you

they will be purchasing now or in the future.

Who Are Your Customers

THE TRENDSETTER
Wigs are like outfits to her! She just loves to look different! Every occasion requires a different slay!
PAIN POINT: She doesn't want to wear the same look. She would hate to just "Blend in. She is easy to sell to.
THE BOUGIE & BUSY
This woman is super busy but she must stay slayed at all times! She doesn't want to spend long hours in the salon or the mirror. She wants to style & go quickly.
PAIN POINT: She needs a wig that doesn't need a lot of styling.
THE NUBIAN PROTECTOR
This woman LOVESSSS her natural hair and she wants to protect it by any means necessary. Her natural hair is high maintenance, so the wigs are her low maintenance
protective style.
PAIN POINT: She needs a wig that protects her real hair.
THE BALD & THE BEAUTIFUL

This woman is beautiful with or without hair but she prefers to wear wigs. She has either lost her hair due to neglect, illness or alopecia.

PAIN POINT: She may desire a wig that can be applied in the privacy of her own home.

Your wig brand is more than just a name; it's an experience, an identity, and a promise to your customers. By following the strategies and insights in this book, you'll be well-equipped to create a compelling and memorable brand that resonates with wig enthusiasts worldwide. Whether you're starting from scratch or looking to revamp your existing brand, remember that effective branding is the key to unlocking success in the ever-evolving world of wigs.

With a strong brand, you can not only capture the hearts of your customers but also leave an indelible mark in the wig industry. So, let's begin the journey to craft a brand that truly sets your wigs apart and makes your business a beacon of style, quality, and innovation.

Social Media Marketing

INSTAGRAM

Study the videos that you are attracted to...duplicate the process with your own personal touch. IG Reels are winning right now, and some creators are getting paid when the post.

TIKTOK

Use the popular songs/challenges when creating videos and again see what is your

particular audience is attracted to and recreate it! Tiktok has made many businesses go viral very easily.

PINTEREST

Tons of ppl go to Pinterest for inspiration. Be their inspiration! Share your work from each of your social media accounts after you post.

FACEBOOK

Most people have the most success with marketing on Facebook by creating reels.

In anything that you do, you must stay CONSISTENT!

When taking photos or recording videos, post the best angle of your finished work. You should snap as many photos as possible so that you have a lot of photos/videos to choose from.

Invest in a Ring light. Lighting is very important. When recording videos, just record! You can edit it later.

Chapter 3 Pricing Your Wigs and Hair

Pricing your wigs effectively is crucial to the success of your wig-making business. It involves a balance between covering your costs, ensuring profitability, and remaining competitive in the market. Here's a step-by-step guide on how to price your wigs:

1. Calculate Your Costs:

Determine the cost of materials, including wig caps, hair, lace, adhesives, and any additional accessories. Factor in overhead costs, such as rent, utilities, equipment, and maintenance.

Include labor costs, accounting for the time spent on wig creation, styling, and customization.

Consider shipping and packaging expenses.

2. Set a Profit Margin:

Decide on a reasonable profit margin. This margin will vary depending on factors like your brand's reputation, quality of wigs, and your target market.

A common profit margin range for handmade wigs is 50% to 100% or more, but it can vary.

3. Research Competitor Pricing:

Study the pricing of similar wigs in the market. Analyze both online and offline competitors. Consider the quality, materials used, and any additional services they offer to justify their prices.

4. Determine Your Unique Selling Proposition (USP):

Identify what makes your wigs stand out. Is it superior quality, unique designs, customizations, or excellent customer service? Use your USP to justify premium pricing if applicable.

5. Account for Customizations:

If you offer customization options like hair type, color, length, or cap size, consider charging extra for these services.

6. Consider Seasonal Trends:

Be flexible with your pricing to accommodate seasonal demand. For instance, you might charge more for holiday-themed wigs during specific times of the year.

7. Test Different Price Points:

Experiment with different price points and monitor sales. This helps you identify the optimal balance between profit and demand.

8. Create Pricing Tiers:

Offer a range of wigs at different price points to cater to a wider audience.

9. Offer Discounts and Promotions:

Run occasional sales or promotions to attract new customers and retain existing ones.

10. Monitor and Adjust:

Regularly review your pricing strategy based on customer feedback, market trends, and

changes in costs.

Don't be afraid to adjust your prices if necessary to stay competitive and profitable.

11. Build Value Through Marketing:

Use effective marketing and branding to create a perception of value for your wigs, allowing you to command higher prices.

12. Transparency:

Clearly communicate your pricing, including any additional charges for customizations or add-ons, to avoid surprises for customers.

*Remember that pricing is not a static process. It's an ongoing effort that requires monitoring and adaptation as your business evolves. Continuously assess your costs, market trends, and customer feedback to ensure your pricing remains competitive and profitable while delivering value to your customers.

Pricing Hack

It's time to talk profit margins – specifically, the kind that can transform your wig-making business. We've uncovered an exciting opportunity that can substantially increase your bottom line: shorter wigs.

Here's the secret: Many wig vendors price their products based on length, which means shorter wigs often come with lower material costs. However, the real magic happens when you realize that customers happily pay for style, not just length. That's where you come in.

By focusing on crafting alluring styles with shorter wigs, you're not only lowering your production costs but also capitalizing on a market that craves trendy, convenient options.

Think about it – stylish bobs, sophisticated pixie cuts, and attention-grabbing asymmetrical designs.

The result? Bigger profit margins for you.

Imagine the impact on your business when you consistently offer fashionable, budget-friendly styles with shorter wigs. You're not just meeting your customers' desires; you're exceeding them while padding your profit margins.

This is the moment to seize the opportunity to make your wig-making venture even more lucrative. Short wigs mean big style, and even bigger profit margins.

So, harness your creative talent, craft those irresistible styles, and watch your profits soar.

Your customers will adore the chic, hassle-free options, and your bank account will reflect your smart business decisions.

Get ready to reap the rewards of bigger profit margins with shorter wigs. It's a game-changer!

Remember, pricing isn't just about numbers; it's a strategic element of your wig-making business. By now, you've learned how to:

Calculate Costs: Accurately assess the expenses that go into crafting each wig.

Set Profit Margins: Determine your desired profit margins to achieve financial success.

Research Competitors: Understand your market and position your prices effectively.

Adapt to Trends: Stay agile and adjust your pricing to seasonal and market trends.

Create Value: Highlight the value your wigs offer to justify your prices.

Build Trust: Maintain transparency to build trust with your customers.

As you embark on your wig-making journey, armed with the knowledge from this book, you can approach pricing with confidence. Remember that pricing is dynamic, and it's okay to adjust your strategies as your business evolves.

Your wigs are more than just hairpieces; they're expressions of style, beauty, and individuality.

With the right pricing strategies, you're not just selling wigs; you're creating the looks!

Chapter 4 No Money Hair and Wigs & Free Amazon Wigs

Many entrepreneurs become focused on buying tons of inventory, buying pretty packaging and spending unnecessary money in the beginning. This won't help your pockets at all!

Your goal is not to sit on tons of inventory that may or may not sell. Your goal is to make continuous sales using as little money as possible. Once your wigs are in demand, take the money you make and properly expand your business!

Here are a few ways to get started as a hairstylist, wig maker or just an entrepreneur selling wigs.

NO INVENTORY NECESSARY

HAIR STYLIST

Create wigs for your clients using their old bundles, closures and/or frontals. Make

sure you document the before and after process for social media footage. Also ask

your client to shout you out on social media when they wear the wig and to refer

anyone who asks about their wig to you (and don't tell 'em it was free).

Take the same approach as the hairstylist but substitute the clients with family,friends and your social network.

Make sure you take time to repair the hair and make the wig look brand new!

. . . .

WIG MAKER

Take the same approach as the hairstylist but substitute the clients with family, friends and your social network.

WIG RETAILER

Don't make wigs? Just want to sell them? Before you start promoting wigs, it would be a great idea to purchase a reputable vendors list or if you've tried hair in the past from a vendor that you really like, you can use the following process too.

Explain to the vendor that you're starting a wig business, and you need photos/videos of their wigs. Be specific about what type of videos or photos you want. (Shaking the hair, rubbing the hair etc.) Reach out to your network and let them know that you're selling wigs. This way may be a little tougher to get started because you don't have hair on hand but you could offer your friends an "introductory price "(the price you pay w| a little extra) just to model your hair. Make them pay you first, then order the hair. Use the vendor photos on your site/social media to promote. Once someone places an order, purchase the hair with their money and keep your profit. Reach out to hairstylists in your area, sell them the hair for a low price, encourage them to sell it to their client at your retail price (higher price) they'll be grateful! You just gave the stylist an opportunity to make extra money and in return ask for video/photo footage of the finished look.

WIG DEALER: HOW TO START YOUR WIG BUSINESS

How To Get Free Wigs from Amazon & Get Paid Doing It!

In the world of online shopping, Amazon stands as a retail giant, oering an array of products, including wigs of all styles and varieties. What if we told you there's a way not only to score free wigs but also to turn this pursuit into a source of income? This guide reveals the secrets to obtaining free wigs from Amazon and harnessing the power of product reviews to earn money along the way. So, if you're ready to dive into a world where freebies and earnings meet, let's embark on this exciting journey together.

Step 1: Create a Wishlist

● Create an Amazon Account: If you don't already have one, create an Amazon account.

● Browse Wigs: Go to Amazon's website and search for wigs you are interested in.

● Add to Wishlist: On the product page of the wigs you like, click the "Add to Wishlist" button. This will save the wigs to your Amazon Wishlist.

Step 2: Contact Sellers

● Find Sellers: Look for sellers on Amazon who are offering the wigs you've added to your Wishlist. You can usually find this information on the product page under "Sold by" or "Fulfilled by."

● Reach Out: Contact the sellers via Amazon's messaging system or email if they have provided contact information. Introduce yourself and express your interest in their wigs.

* Most have had a lot of success by reaching out to these sellers through Instagram. If it's easier for you, search hashtags like #amazonwigs or simply search amazon wigs and find sellers on Instagram, send them a DM!

Here are two newbie-friendly vendors I've had positive experiences with:

@pikjade_human_hair_wigs

@adronite_hair_ocial

There's an abundance of them on Instagram!

*Sellers may ask for you to pay half of the wigs cost upfront and they'll refund your money back to you through PayPal once you leave the review on amazon.

Step 3: Offer to Review

• Propose a Review: In your message to the seller, offer to write a detailed and honest review of their wig in exchange for a free or discounted wig. Explain that you are an enthusiastic Amazon customer and can provide valuable feedback.

• Highlight Your Profile: Mention your Amazon profile and any previous reviews you've written. Sellers are more likely to provide products to customers who actively engage with a platform.

• Be Professional: Be courteous and professional in your communication with sellers. Make sure your request is clear and concise. If you want a free wig...just say that!

Step 4: Wait for a Response Patience is Key: Sellers may take some time to respond to your request, so be patient.

Step 5: Fulfill Your End of the Bargain

• Receive the Wig: If the seller agrees, they will send you the wig.

• Write a Detailed Review: Once you receive the wig, thoroughly test it and write a

detailed review on Amazon. Include both positive aspects and constructive criticism if applicable. Be honest and objective.

Step 6: Maintain a Good Relationship

Stay in Touch: Keep communication open with the seller, and if you are satisfied with their product and service, express your interest in reviewing more of their products in the future.

It's important to note that not all sellers may agree to provide free wigs in exchange for reviews, and Amazon's policies regarding product reviews can change. Always ensure that you follow Amazon's guidelines and maintain transparency in your reviews to build trust with sellers and other customers.

WIG DEALER: HOW TO START YOUR WIG BUSINESS

Now, since we all cherish the allure of freebies, whether it's about saving a few bucks or turning the tables to earn more coins Become an Amazon Influencer! This strategy lets you earn a commission from every wig that's sold on your storefront. Even better, if your followers click on your link to buy a wig but end up purchasing other items, you'll still make money o their purchase because they're within your

referral link! It's a win win!

To get started, follow these steps:

● Visit the Amazon Influencer Program sign-up page at

https://aliate-program.amazon.com/influencers

● Complete the sign-up process, creating your Amazon influencer profile.

● Make sure you copy & save your amazon storefront link so that you can share it on your social media profiles.

Now here's how to make some extra coins without being an amazon influencer...

This is your golden ticket to make some extra coins. Some women buy these same wigs and pay a stylist to install and style them. If you are a wig designer/stylist, take these free wigs, add your styling magic, make them glueless, and sell them for 100% profit. No middleman (other stylist) required!

Ready to embark on this exciting journey to free wigs and boundless possibilities? Let's get started!"

Chapter 5 Wig Color Formulas

. . . .

IN THIS SECTION YOU will find color formulas for your wigs and hair. See Attached Photos for Permanent and Semi- Permanent Colors along with Color Combinations.

Adore Semi Permanent Colors

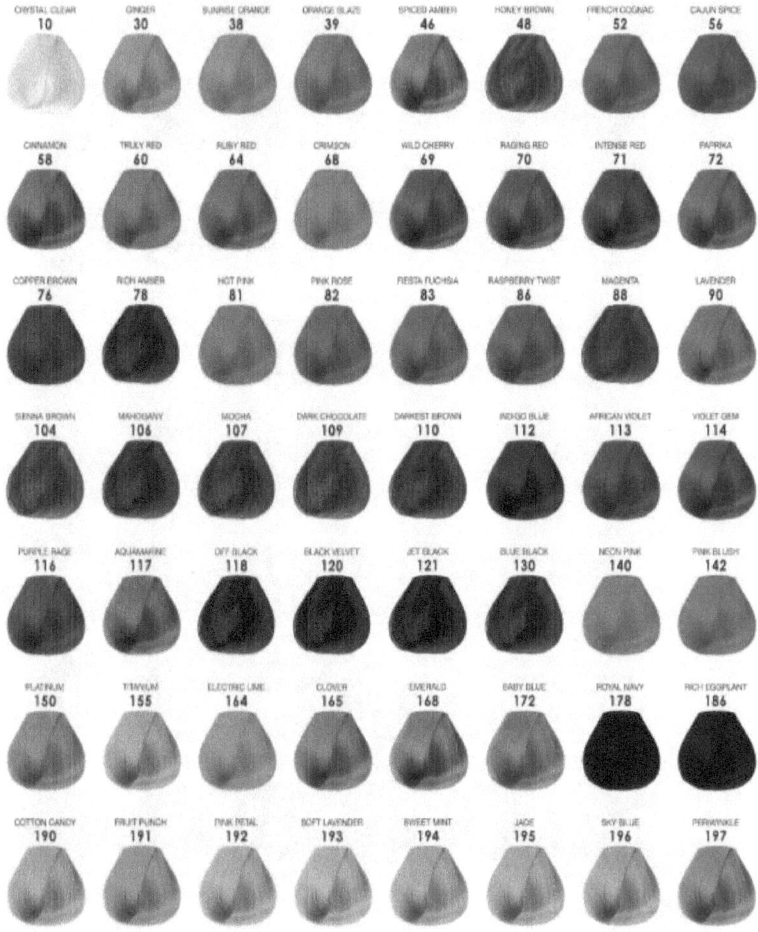

Kiss Colors Tintation

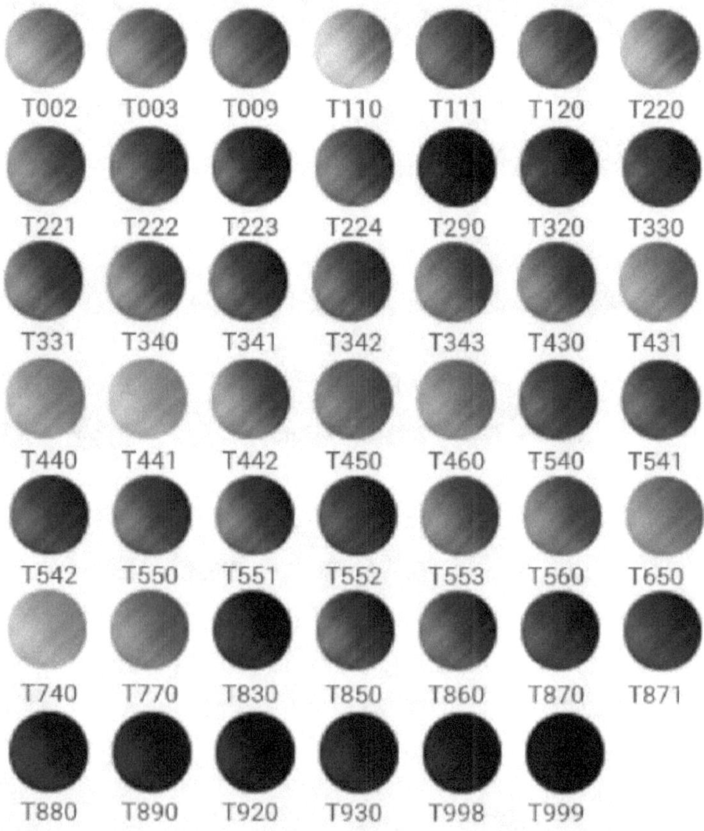

Kiss Colors Express
SEMI PERMANENT

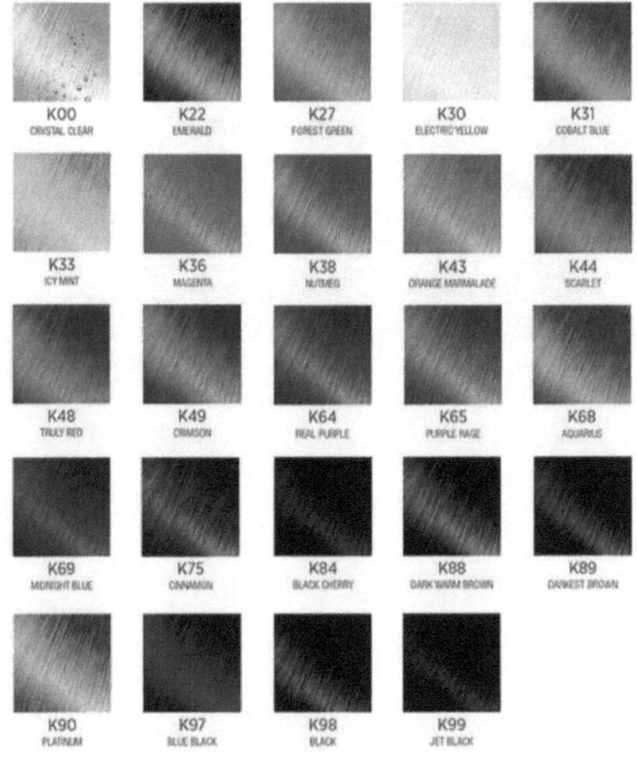

Joico Intensity

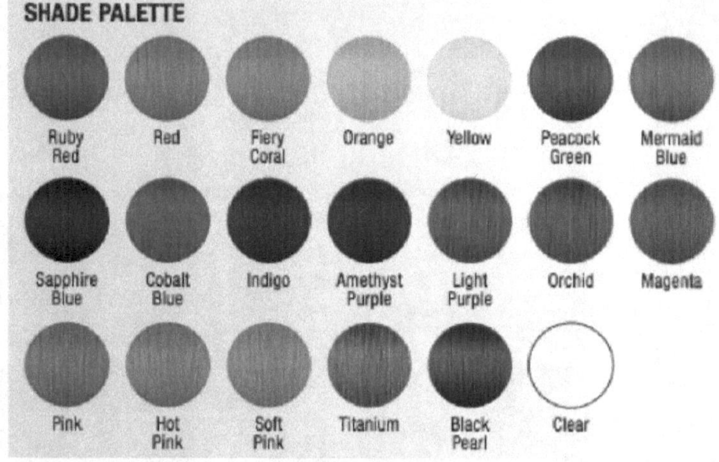

Wigs & Colors
TIPS & TRICKS

Achieve vibrant colors using 613 hair and wigs. DO NOT try to lighten dark hair to acheive these colors. Its a waste of time and it will be a waste of hair. Trust me.

Semi Permanent Hair Color DOES NOT alter the structure of the hair. So if the hair goes bad after you color it...it was bad to begin with. Its not the color

Water Coloring is a quick and easy way to color hair. If you decide to use water coloring, use Adore and paint the roots with a color brush instead of dipping the roots in the water to prevent coloring the knots

Mix Purple Shampoo (Joico or Shimmering Lights) with water to remove the yellow from 613 hair. Soak the hair for 20 mins

Shampoo & dry(613) hair before coloring for better results

Wig Coloring

THE HAIRLINE
The most imoprtant area

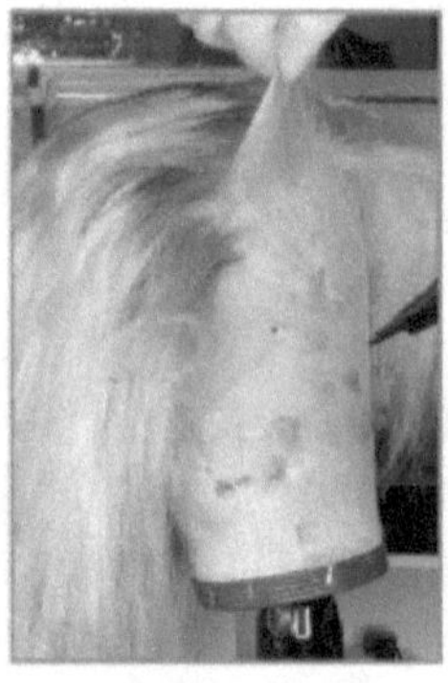

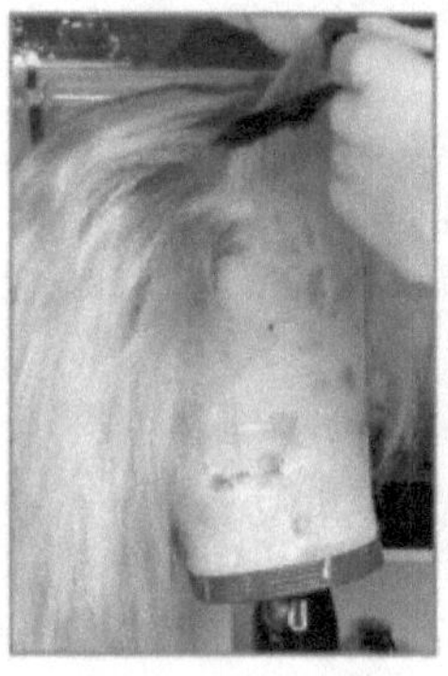

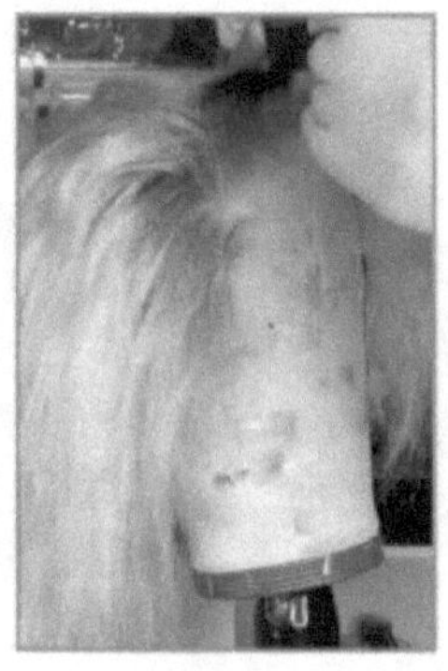

PULL HAIR STRAIGHT UP AND AWAY FROM THE LACE USING MINIMUM TENSION

PLACE THE COLOR ABOUT AN INCH AWAY FROM THE ROOTS

ONCE MOST OF THE COLOR HAS BEEN TRANSFERRED FROM THE BRUSH TO THE HAIR,USE THE COLOR "RESIDUE" TO COLOR THE ROOTS . THIS PREVENTS COLOR FROM DRIPPING ON THE LACE

Wig Coloring

PROTECT THE LACE

HOLD THE HAIR STRAIGHT OUT FROM THE LACE. PAINT THE ROOTS LAST USING THE LEFT OVER COLOR "RESIDUE' ON THE BRUSH.THIS PREVENTS COLOR FROM DRIPPING ON TO THE LACE

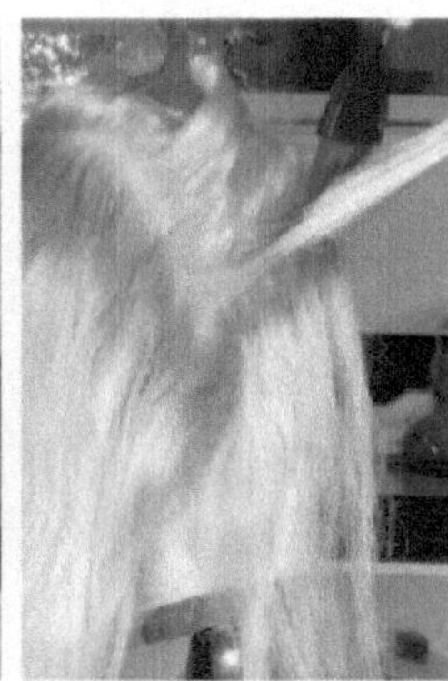

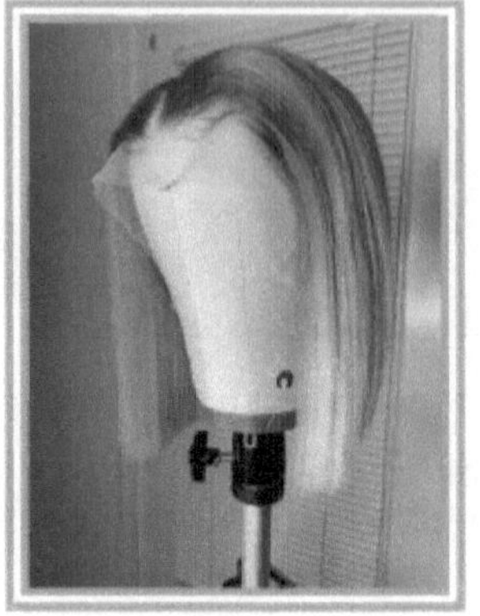

COLOR FORMULA:

- **KISS PURPLE PASSION**
- **ADORE JADE**
- **KISS LIMELIGHT**
- **ADORE NEON PINK**
- **ADORE ORANGE BLAZE**

VENDOR:
ROCKIN HAIR
PRODUCTS

HAIR LENGTH:
14 INCHES

HAIR TEXTURE:
613 BODY WAVE

Left Side: Mix Adore Neon Pink w Kiss Purple 2:1 to create a root color .After you've applied the root color, apply neon pink to the midsection of the hair and Orange Blaze to the ends. Right Side: apply Kiss Purple passion to the roots, Jade to the midsection and Limelight to the ends

RIGHT SIDE: LEFT SIDE:

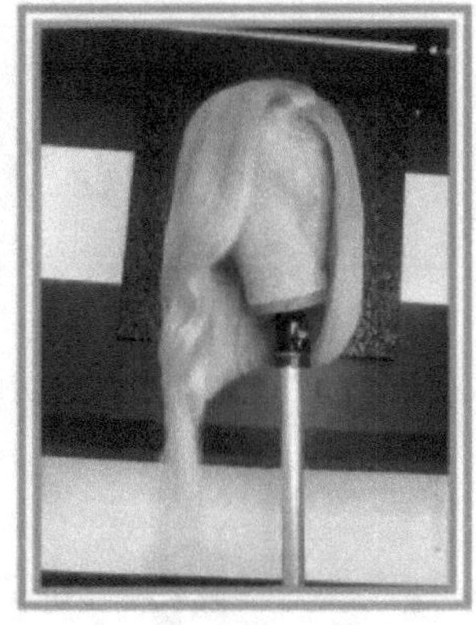

VENDOR:
ROCKIN HAIR
PRODUCTS

HAIR LENGTH:
18 INCHES

HAIR TEXTURE:
613 BODY WAVE

COLOR FORMULA:

- **ADORE PINK ROSE**
- **ADORE VIOLET GEM**
- **PINK PETAL**
- **PLATINUM**

MIX PINK ROSE & VIOLET GEM (2:1) ND APPLY TO THE ROOTS. APPLY PINK PETAL TO THE MIDSHAFT (MIDDLE STRANDS) AND DILUTED PLATINUM TO THE ENDS.

*PLATINUM CAN BE MIXED WITH WATER 1:1

Stormi Rain

COLOR FORMULA:

- **ADORE PERIWINKLE**
- **ADORE JADE**

VENDOR:
ROCKIN HAIR
PRODUCTS

HAIR LENGTH:
14 INCHES

HAIR TEXTURE:
613 BODY WAVE

SHAMPOO THE HAIR WITH A PURPLE SHAMPOO TO REMOVE THE YELLOW. CONDITION AND DRY. PART THE HAIR ON YOUR DESIRED SIDE. CONTINUE PARTING AND MAKE THE SECTION A 4X4 SQUARE AREA(THIS WILL BE THE HEAVY BANG AREA) . CLIP IT OUT THE WAY. MIX ADORE PERIWINKLE W/ WATER IN A SINK SIZE BOWL FILLED WITH 1/4 WATER. WATER COLOR THE AREA THAT IS UNPINNED. AFTER,TAKE ONE INCH PARTINGS IN THE 4X4 PINNED AREA AND ALTERNATE COLORS ON EACH SECTION WITH JADE AND PERIWINKLE

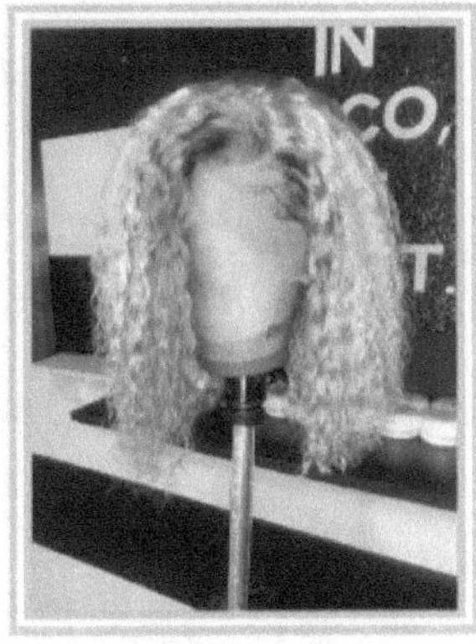

VENDOR:
NEW ONE HAIR

HAIR LENGTH:
16 INCHES

HAIR TEXTURE:
613 DEEP WAVE

COLOR FORMULA:

- **ADORE JADE**
- **ADORE PINK**
  BLUSH
- **LAVENDER**
- **PINK PETAL**

Shampoo the hair with Joico shampoo to remove the yellow.
Condition & Dry. On a small section of hair color the roots Blush Pink
and the midshaft Jade or Lavender.or pink petal Alternate colors. BE
creative!

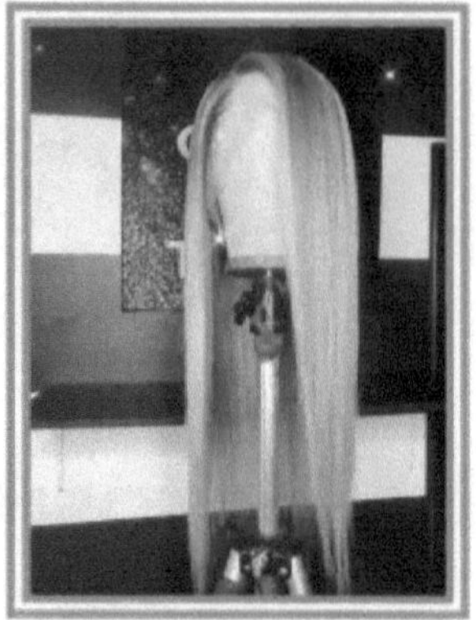

COLOR FORMULA:

- ## ADORE ROYAL NAVY
- ## LAVENDER
- ## JADE

VENDOR:
DIAMOND VIRGIN HAIR

HAIR LENGTH:
24 INCHES FULL LACE

HAIR TEXTURE:
613 STRAIGHT

COLOR THE ROOTS ROYAL NAVY. THEN SECTION THE HAIR INTO 3 INCH BLOCKS, ONE BLOCK IS COLORED LAVENDER. THE NEXT BLOCK IS NOT COLORED, THE NEXT BLOCK IS JADE.

(REFER TO THE VIDEO FOR MY COLOR PLACEMENT) OF THE OTHER COLORS...OR JUST FREE STYLE AND BE CREATIVE!

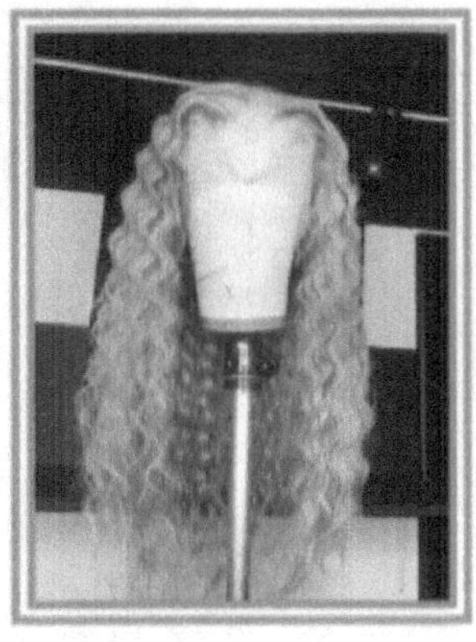

Vendor:
Rockin Hair Products

Hair Length:
24 inches full lace

Hair Texture:
613 Body Wave

COLOR FORMULA:

- **ADORE PERIWINKLE ADORE JADE**
- **ADORE ORANGE BLAZE**
- **KISS ELECTRIC YELLLOW**

THIS A RANDOM CREATIVE COLOR. THE ROOTS WERE COLORED PERIWINKLE & JADE. THE MIDDLE SECTION AND ENDS WERE COLORED WITH PINK PETAL, ORANGE BLAZE & ELECTRIC YELLOW

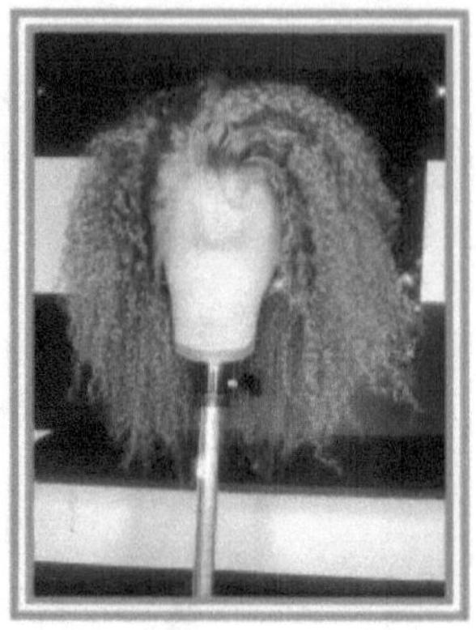

Sandy Brulee

VENDOR:
ROCKIN HAIR
PRODUCTS

HAIR LENGTH:
16INCH FRONTAL &
THREE 16 INCH BUNDLES

HAIR TEXTURE:
NATURAL COLORED
KINKY CURLY

COLOR FORMULA:

- **BLONDOR**
- **30 VOL DEVELOPER**

MIX BLONDOR LIGHTENER AND 40 VOL DEVELOPER OR ANY LIGHTENER YOU CHOOSE. BRUSH THIS HAIR OUT WITH A PADDLE BRUSH. APPLY THE LIGHTNER MIXTURE TO THE HAIR, PLACE THE WIG IN A PLASTIC BAG AND LET IT PROCESS FOR 25-30 MINS FRONTAL: DYE THE HAIR 1/2 INCH WAY FROM THE LACE. DYE THE ROOT ARE LAST.

Jamaican Love

VENDOR:
ROCKIN HAIR
PRODUCTS

HAIR LENGTH:
24 INCHES

HAIR TEXTURE:
NATURAL COLORED
LOOSE WAVE

COLOR FORMULA:

- **ADORE PAPRIKA**
- **KISS FOREST GREEN**
- **KISS ELECTRIC YELLOW**

OMBRE THE HAIR WITH BLONDOR OR BW LIGHTENER AND 40VL DEVELOPER. SHAMPOO,CONDITION AND DRY THE HAIR. PART THE HAIR HORIZONTALLY FROM EAR TO EAR . DYE THE BOTTOM SECTION OF THE LIGHTENED HAIR FOREST GREEN AND DYE THE ENDS ELECTRIC YELLOW. DYE THE TOP SECTION PAPRIKA AND THE ENDS YELLOW

Carli

VENDOR:
ROCKIN HAIR
PRODUCTS

HAIR LENGTH:
10 INCHES FULL LACE

HAIR TEXTURE:
613 BODY WAVE

SHAMPOO WIG WITH JOICO PURPLE
SHAMPOO OR SHIMMERING LIGHTS.
APPLY ADORE ROYAL NAVY TO THE
ROOTS, AND POWDER BLUE TO THE
MIDSHAFT. IF THE SHAMPOO HAS
TONED THE HAIR, TITANIUM DOESNT
HAVE TO BE USED ON THE ENDS. IF THE
ENDS HAVE A YELLOW TINT, USE
TITANIUM

COLOR FORMULA:

- **ADORE ROYAL NAVY**
- **ADORE POWDER BLUE**
- **ADORE TITANIUM OR JOICO PURPLE SHAMPOO**

COLOR FORMULA:

- **ADORE TITANIUM**
- **RUSK DEEPSHINE 1.000NC BLACK**

VENDOR:
TRUSCEND HAIR

HAIR LENGTH:
12INCH 613 RONTAL &
THREE 12INCH NATURAL
BUNDLES

HAIR TEXTURE:
BODY WAVE

THE FRONTAL IS A 613 (BLONDE) FRONTAL. THE BUNDLES ARE A NATURAL BROWN. DYE THE FRONTAL WITH THE ADORE TITANIUM AND OMBRE THE ENDS OF THE FRONTAL WITH A PERMANENT BLACK . DYE THE BUNDLES BLACK ALSO

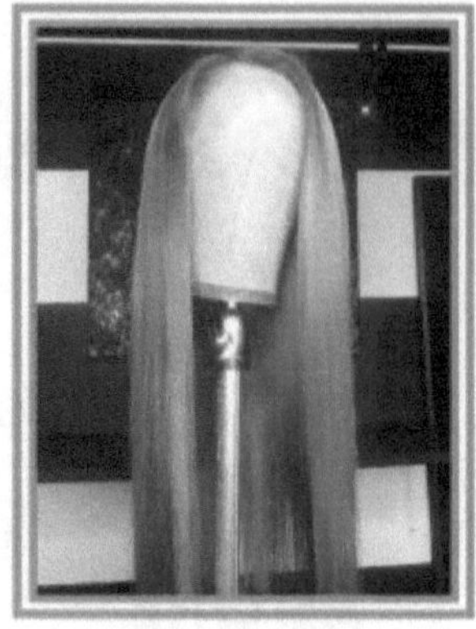

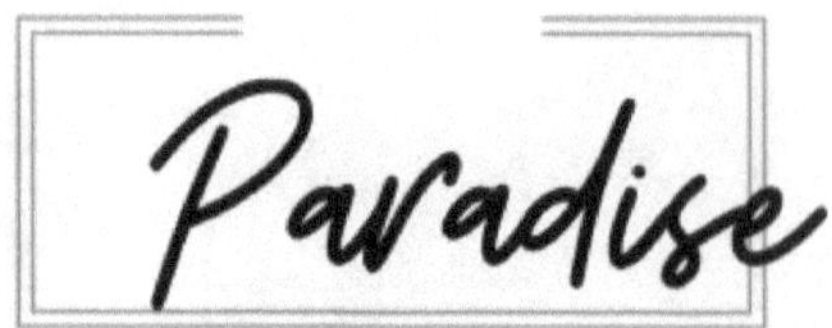

VENDOR:
WHITE LABEL HAIR

HAIR LENGTH:
24 INCH FULL LACE WIG

HAIR TEXTURE:
STRAIGHT

COLOR FORMULA:

- **KISS MAGENTA**
- **KISS MIDNIGHT BLUE**
- **KISS ELECTRIC YELLOW**
- **KISS COBALT BLUE**
- **KISS ORANGE MARMALADE**

REFER TO THE VIDEO FOR COLOR PLACEMENT

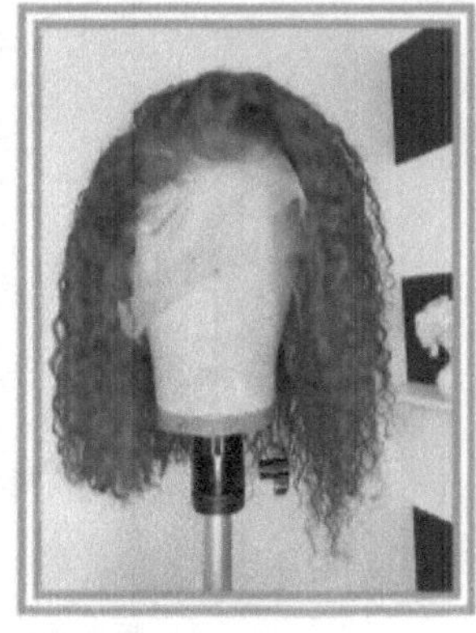

COLOR FORMULA:

VENDOR:
NEW ONE HAIR

HAIR LENGTH:
141 INCH FULL LACE

HAIR TEXTURE:
613 DEEPWAVE

2 TUBES OF JOICO INTENSITY MAGENTA

PRE WASH THE HAIR. DRY & ADD COLOR

VENDOR:
ROCKIN HAIR
PRODUCTS

HAIR LENGTH:
14 INCH FULL LACE

HAIR TEXTURE:
613 STRAIGHT

COLOR FORMULA:

- **ADORE LAVENDER**
- **KISS ELECTRIC YELLOW**
- **ADORE JADE**
- **ADORE BLUSH PINK**
- **ADORE SUNSET ORANGE**

EACH COLORED SECTION IS COLORED WITH TWO COLORS. EXAMPLE :ROOT TO MID AREA IS YELLOWAND ENDS ARE PINK. ROOT AREA IN ANOTHER SECTION IS LAVENDER AND ENDS ARE ORANGE. GET CREATIVE!

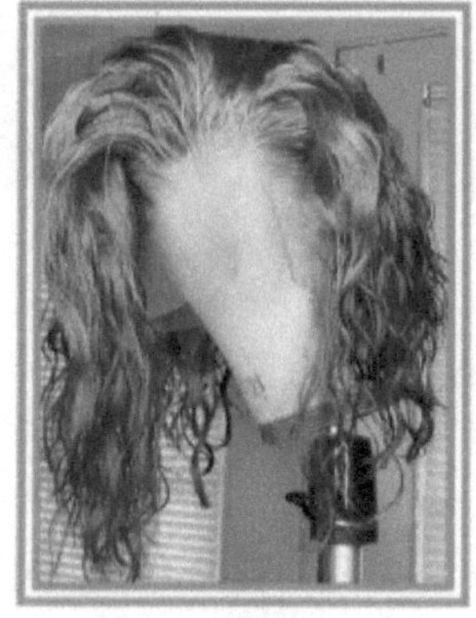

VENDOR:
ROCKIN HAIR
PRODUCTS

HAIR LENGTH:
14 INCH LACE FRONTAL

HAIR TEXTURE:
613 BODYWAVE

Oceana

COLOR FORMULA:

- ## ADORE ROYAL NAVY

PRE-WASH THE HAIR WITH A PURPLE SHAMPOO TO REMOVE THE YELLOW. ADD A SMALL AMOUNT OF ADORE ROYAL NAVY TO A SINK OR SINK SIZED BOWL FILLED WITH SEMI HOT WATER. DIP A PIECE OF PAPER IN THE WATER TO ENSURE THAT THE WATERCOLOR IS NOT TOO DARK. IF IT IS, ADD MORE WATER. ONCE YOU DIP THE ENTIRE WIG, ADD MORE ROYAL NAVY TO THE WATER. MAKE IT A SHADE DARKER. DIP THE ENDS. TOWEL DRY. PLACE THE WIG ON YOUR CANVAS HEAD. TURN IT UPSIDE DOWN, SHAKE IT AND SCRUNCH THE ENDS. AIR DRY OR PLACE UNDER DRYER

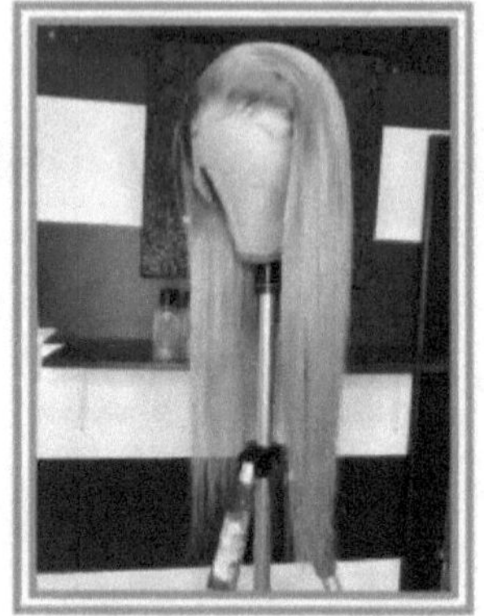

Rainbow Denim

VENDOR:
ROCKIN HAIR
PRODUCTS

HAIR LENGTH:
24 INCH FULL LACE

HAIR TEXTURE:
613 STRAIGHT

COLOR FORMULA:

- **ADORE POWDER BLUE**
- **KISS ORANGE**
- **KISS ELECTRIC YELLOW**
- **KISS MAGENTA**
- **KISS COBALT BLUE**

UPDATED COLORS. SOME COLORS WERE BETTER THAN WHAT WAS ORINALLY USED

THIS IS A FORM OF CREATIVE COLORING. EACH SECTION HAS 3 COLORS PER SECTION. FOR EXAMPLE, MAGENTA ROOTS, COBALT BLUE MIDSECTION & YELLOW ENDS. THE NEXT SECTION MAY HAVE ORANGE ROOTS, YELLOW MIDSECTION AND MAGENTA ENDS

Just Remember

GET CREATIVE! YOU CANT MESS THIS UP!

YOU'LL BEGIN TO DEVELOP YOUR OWN TECHNIQUES AND COLOR PLACEMENTS ALONG THE WAY. RECORD IT AND DOCUMENT IT

IF YOU FEEL LIKE YOU'VE MESSEDUP. GIVE IT A CUTE STYLE, SHOW IT TO YOUR AUDIENCE. THEY WILL NOT KNOW HE DIFFERENCE. TRUST ME, IT WILL GET SOLD!

Chapter 6 High Quality Wig and Hair Vendors

Https://www.privatelabelextensions.com/[1]
https://www.allovehair.com/
https://www.minkhairweave.com/
https://ballicevirginhair.com/
https://www.hairsmarket.com/
https://www.kabeilu.com/
https://www.tedhair.com/
https://www.nadula.com/
https://prarvihair.com/
https://www.rebehair.com/
Whatsapp +86 136 6013 1362 (ANNA)
Whatsapp +86 138 2213 2594 (LILLIAN)
Whatsapp +86 138 2213 2514 (FANCY)
Whatsapp +86 181 0261 2204 (SHEETA)

For the numbers on Whatsapp let them know you are a reseller and want to do business with them. Also let them know you would like to see their inventory, ask for prices, shipping time, packaging etc. Keep in mind they are on a different time zone so give them time to answer

Your goal is to build relationships with your vendors. These are the people that

are going to Help your business run as smoothly as possible. Once you decide to do

business with a vendor, they are officially on your team!

when reaching out to VENDORS on WhatsApp, introduce yourself and tell them about your business.

They Know their product & THEY KNOW THE MARKET SO ASK QUESTIONS!

---

1. https://www.privatelabelextensions.com/

WIG DEALER: HOW TO START YOUR WIG BUSINESS

REMEMBER...THE VENDORS DAY TIME Is our nighttime and vice versa so you may want to reach out to them Late in the evening.

FYI: Most of the vendors are using their own cell phones so once you build a relationship, they'll reply to you on their off days too!

Each one of these vendors have a VARIETY of quality wigs & bundles.

Custom Wig Units

This Vendor will create a frontal/Closure wig unit for you, Choose a Frontal or Closure, bundles in different lengths, Cap size and Cap type. The

fee starts at $15 & up. They will also add an extra band free of charge. They

also sell a variety of Full lace wigs, lace frontal wigs, bundles and HD Frontals & closures

Company: Truscend Virgin Hair Sales Rep:Victor

Website: Truscend.com

Instagram: truscendvirginhair_victor

WhatsApp: +8615089833867

613 Wigs & HD LACE

This Wig Vendor has some great quality & Affordable 613 Full Lace Wigs.

They also have full lace wigs without the band for customization of the nape area. They also sell HD LACE NOW!

Company: Rockin Hair Products

Sales Rep: Micheal

Website: Rockinhairproducts.com

Instagram:virgin_hair.factory

WhatsApp: +8618661694029

US(Atlanta) Wig Vendor (virgin & 613)

This Wig Vendor sells a variety of Full Lace wigs. They offer low cost shipping and drop shipping. They can create and house your packaging.

Once your customer places an order, they will ship the wigs right to your customer with your company information on the packaging.
Company: Berrys fashion hair Instagram:@berrysfashionhairusa
WhatsApp:
+4704089437
HD LACE (613 WIG)
HD LACE ON A 613 WIGS, Frontals &Closures
Company: Echo hair
Sales Rep:ECHO
Instagram: @echo_prettyhair
WhatsApp: +8613468287338
HD THIN SWISS LACE
HD THIN SWISS LACE FRONTAL,CLOSURES & WIGS
COMPANY:OPTIMAL HAIR
SALES REP. ROMAN
INSTAGRAM: @OPTIMALHAIR
WHATSAPP:+8618053222386

Chapter 7 Free Shopify Wig Store Themes

• • • •

IN THIS SECTION YOU can access all your Shopify Store Themes and Download to add to your Website. There are several to choose from and the file is big so it may be best to download and send to a PC or laptop.

• • • •

ACCESS YOUR FILES AT:

https://drive.google.com/file/d/
1V0SXVlTWtaPrS_xMGeJsTT8kexsJvzsJ/
view?usp=sharing

Don't miss out!

Visit the website below and you can sign up to receive emails whenever Rachael Reed publishes a new book. There's no charge and no obligation.

https://books2read.com/r/B-A-WXARB-TTHWE

BOOKS2READ

Connecting independent readers to independent writers.

Did you love *Wig Dealer: How to Start Your wig Business*? Then you should read *Can't Turn a Hoe Into a Housewife*[1] by Rachael Reed!

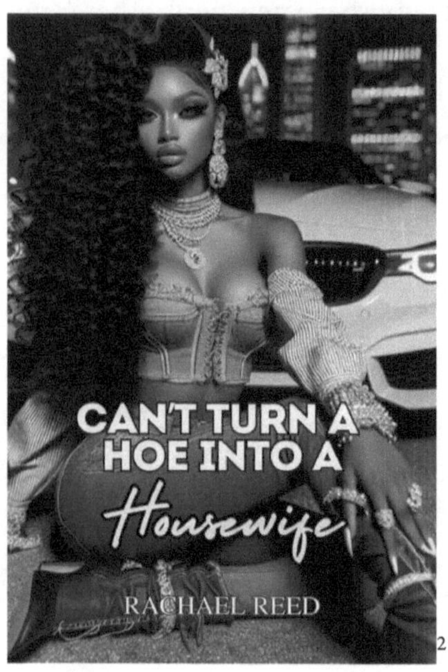

[2]

In the gritty streets of the city, where loyalty is tested and danger lurks around every corner, Can't Turn a Hoe into a Housewife dives deep into the underbelly of urban life. Erica, a seasoned escort with a sharp mind and a guarded heart, dreams of escaping the fast life and finding something real. But in a world where money rules and trust is scarce, her journey ain't easy.

When Erica crosses paths with Quan, a man with a genuine heart and a promise of love, she sees a glimmer of hope. But leaving the game ain't simple, especially with a ruthless pimp like Lil Ron, who ain't about to let his top girl go without a fight. As Erica tries to walk the line

---

1. https://books2read.com/u/4XdEN1

2. https://books2read.com/u/4XdEN1

between her old life and a new beginning, Lil Ron tightens his grip, turning their lives into a deadly game of cat and mouse.

Can't Turn a Hoe into a Housewife is a tale of love, betrayal, and survival in a world where the streets don't play fair. With a dark, raw tone and a cast of characters struggling against their circumstances, this story is packed with twists, drama, and the harsh reality of street life. As Erica fights to break free and find redemption, the stakes get higher, and the danger becomes all too real.

In this urban fiction thriller, the line between right and wrong blurs, and every choice comes with a price. Will Erica escape the life that's bound her, or will the streets claim her for good? Get ready for a cliffhanging ride through the hood, where love ain't always enough to save you from your past.

Also by Rachael Reed

Sis
Sis 2 Blood on the Streets

Standalone
Codefendant
Codefendant
Once a Cheater
Once a Cheater
Passport Bro
What Happens in Prison
Preference
Sprinkle Sprinkle
Championship Bad
Street Exodus
Street Exodus
Street Royalty
Pawns of Power
SIS
Cartel Bloodline
Get Money Girls
Skip the Games
Til Death Do Us Part

Backpage Hustle
Link in Bio
The Virgin and The Kingpin
A Gangsta's Heart
Boosters
Can't Turn a Hoe Into a Housewife
Better you Than Me
Wig Dealer: How to Start Your wig Business